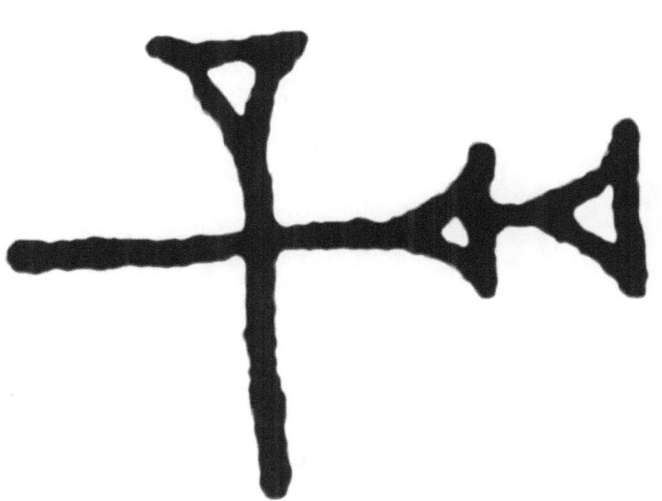

How Marijuana Will Save the World

The Cultural Criticism of an Unhappy Citizen

AuthorHouse™
1663 Liberty Drive, Suite 200
Bloomington, IN 47403
www.authorhouse.com
Phone: 1-800-839-8640

First published by AuthorHouse 11/22/2008

ISBN: 978-1-4389-3872-1 (e)
ISBN: 978-1-4389-3002-2 (sc)

Printed in the United States of America
Bloomington, Indiana

This book is printed on acid-free paper.

The following may or may not be a fictional account:

Tiny hairs mask an absurd creation
of my willingness to forego any sort
of public response to what has gutted
me from inside to out. Yes, you have
no idea what is happening in the
depths of the hell burning in my eyes
but let me tell you that when it
envelops us all, only god's tears will
wash and purge me from this prison.
Teenage girls have nothing on my
inability to dream. I stole everything
to become what I am, a monk
realizing the illusion (or delusion) he
has slipped into is just that—a waste
of life. Electricity is flipped and now
this energy is nothing for you...

i

<u>Foreword</u>

In between the various episodes of oppressive brutality, a child will often develop a unique understanding with which to make sense of the world: that which is loved and that which is hated becomes fused together to create the essence of a new totality of mind. It is in this synthesized epitome of consciousness and heightened state of awareness that a child is given the opportunity to translate his and her theory for the world, by and through action, after which he and she are judged accordingly.

Yet it is precisely this judgment that provides the inherent failing and fundamental contradiction for the child, whereby he and she are either accepted into the community or cast out into exile. To be rendered "useless," or even to be declared as "wrong" would be to presume an infallible and outside authority, of which all things, great and small, would be held accountable to in a specific acknowledgement of what is, in fact, determined to be "good," leaving no alternative but to do what is expected.

This book brings the story of a prisoner's theory and justification for action together with the curse of a rationale that maintains his and her displacement within a dominant society. One self-described magician, The Author, journeys into the heart of darkness in order to better understand his and her own place in a spatial and temporal world—one of subjugation in a milieu of political and economic (and environmental and cultural) violence that borders on the genocide and extermination of an entire population.

For my parents,

And the ones I will never stop loving

Have you learned to speak yet? With bright colors dripping from dark lips, teeth straining despair like orange pulp? Because I haven't. I haven't risen from this. A desk faces the front of an empty classroom...where is my teacher?

Preface

Part One:

The Universal Organism Known as Fate

"This great feeding body is the world. It evolved together, mutually, all interdependent, all interrelating ceaselessly, the dust of old stars hurtling through time, and we are the form it chose to make it conscious of itself."

-Jack Turner

To resist a system, whether colonization, globalization, or the general militarization of an imposed ideology, is to resist the evolution of time. It becomes a resistance to "progression," in that there exists no tolerance for dissent in a previously established system, which itself becomes static before collapsing. Revolution, on the other hand, is the rejection of the "law" of a status quo, in the attempt to assert oneself and be recognized as "acceptable" by the system. In this way, the continuous presence of revolution over time becomes the evolution of an organism to be called fate. This helps us differentiate between Resistance and Revolution, while providing a new framework for understanding the actions and mindsets of any character in one of their various narratives.

Many times, the reader will be presented with a child who must battle the conditions he and she are subjected to in order to survive. There can be no resistance at any point, but rather, the reader will witness the total submission of the child to any and all events that transpire. Any resistance would result in the death of the character at the hands of those who maintain the oppressive system, and so, each step the child takes to survive becomes its own revolution against the assumed extermination that is projected to occur.

In dealing with any and all atrocities, it is important to remember that these events have all been predetermined by "god," or rather, "the will of god," or rather, "fate," or rather, all previous situations that have directly contributed to the atrocity itself. This helps us to contextualize the atrocity as nothing more than a new present, void of any subjectivity, for us to form a new paradigm in which to create a new future. Only by revolting against "god's plan" will we ever maintain a continual system of "freedom," through which we may finally declare ourselves to be the masters of our own destinies. Resistance, however, is futile.

Part Two:

On Tameness

"In Wildness is the preservation of the   World."

-Henry David Thoreau

To tame another is not necessarily to take out or destroy the Wildness that resides within, but rather to instill some recognition that alternatives to those actions deemed "Wild" do in fact exist. For instance, when feeding a pigeon (and similarly a bear) it is important to understand why you are feeding it. If you feed it out of kindness, the animal may consider you to be a viable source for food (in one way or another). This is not to say that it is "bad" to do so, but rather that one should accept and be aware of the consequences and repercussions that accompany the action. To feed an animal for the sole purpose of making it dependent on the feeder, however, is to enslave and control the animal: food is the energy that an animal needs to survive, which will in turn do anything (morally justifiable or not) to attain it to sustain its own life. If an animal's life is self-governed, it is autonomous and so, Wild. If the animal is dependent on others for life, it is forcibly coerced into tameness, with the threat of extermination holding it in its slavery.

With this said, tameness can indeed coexist with Wildness. Once an animal leaves its sphere of Wildness to interact with a human, the ability to be tamed is either learned or instilled. Unfortunately, it is in transcending this boundary between Wildness and Humaneness that has brought up such controversial topics as Wilderness and its role in man's dominion over his surroundings. This detrimental concept prohibits any essence of Wildness from permeating the natural order of the environment as it works under the assumption that Nature is fundamentally apart from the realm of humanness.

Whether we take on the role of "preserver" or "conserver" to keep humans out of the resources we maintain for ourselves, the idea of control is still ever present. Many times, Wilderness preservations are orchestrated and promoted by ex-hunters-turned-conservationists who seek to impose a "western" system of national parks onto developing landscapes. While perhaps beneficial for wealthy political elites, the designation of Nature reserves helps to displace villages and their inhabitants. Places long settled and densely populated with agrarian cultures have a finely balanced relationship with Nature, and the setting aside of Wilderness areas has many times resulted in the direct transfer of resources from the poor to the rich.

When an environment is controlled it is more often than not controlled by those eventually favored within the new system. Yet the establishment of a self-imposed hierarchy of natural order directly contradicts the rationale for which preservations are created in the first place: the transformation of Wildness into Wilderness is demonstrative of the abstraction we attribute to Nature and guides such legislation that would propose to make it illegal for a wolf to eat a deer in the winter or would demand the destruction of a bear who kills and eats (in its own environment) an invading person. By assuming the power to dictate what is and what is not an acceptable food chain, man gains an omnipotence in relation to his surroundings that is perhaps not fully deserved. He has taken himself out of the environment in order to "more effectively" decide for the animals what they are allowed to eat, where they are allowed to go, and in what places they are allowed to reside. By allowing, controlling, and dictating what can, will, and should happen, any Wildness that Nature once enjoyed is suppressed and forgotten as freedom is ultimately destroyed.

It is this logic that tells us that while Wildness is inherent, Wilderness is demarcated to "protect" it from its human counterparts. The Wilderness Act of 1964 reads, "A wilderness, in contrast with those areas where man and his works dominate the landscape, is hereby recognized as an area where the earth and its community of life are untrammeled by man, where man himself is a visitor who does not remain." Besides reinforcing a distinct separateness between man and Nature, the Wilderness concept presupposes that the too few Wilderness reserves created will offset or outweigh all damaging tropical forestry projects, while excusing the violent loss of life that a population of animals, plants, and ecosystems undoubtedly incur. Thus, a Wilderness can never truly be Wild, as the form will always exclude the content. If the animal is relegated to a specific location, though it may retain its own inherent Wildness, the environment certainly cannot. It becomes artificial, kept distinct from a natural progression to be ultimately made tame. The animal is likewise rendered tame, pacified to mirror an environment devoid of any Wildness while becoming dependent on the governed environment and susceptible to the whims of those that govern it. In this instance, the animal has become enslaved to the master of its surroundings and is at His mercy.

Even when tameness overwhelms the animal, Wildness can certainly be recovered. A child may flee from a repressive family and destroyed social life to repossess a Wildness that has long been absent, mutually mutating into an animal to escape a tame environment for one that may eventually kill them. Though perhaps tragic for his and her family and friends, the child's journey documents a spiritual reawakening as he and she discover for their self the Wildness unattained in a previous life. By leaving the sphere of tameness for a sphere of Wildness to coexist within, a child will regain that natural animalistic understanding he and she will often find so beautiful; and though perhaps maintaining an elevated morality compared to an animal, the child will be absorbed back into the natural food cycle to personify firsthand the theme of "Energeia."

Nothing that lives exists except through the ingestion of another's energy, of which not only the edible "other," but rather the complete and total makeup of The Beast will exist as the general history of transferred energy. In this way does food become the affiliation between all beings, revealing the child's soul to be inextricably linked to that energy which he and she choose to ingest, returning them to a natural state of affairs of which he and she are both the ends and the means to. It is in retrieving this sense of harmonious recognition that a child will truly become Wild again.

Environmental ethics must be predicated initially upon basic animal rights (though perhaps the term "animal" is too specific and does not extend to plant life and human life, and should therefore be referred to as Basic Living Systems). These [Basic Living Systems] are first and foremost to be acknowledged as created equally, with mutual respect to each as an afforded understanding. Furthermore, there is certainly a food chain, food being the energy needed and chosen to maintain a life system. With this consideration do we begin to carve out an ethic regarding Land.

Being more than merely "the ground," Land acts as a fountain of energy to produce a food chain, conducted through a circuit of soil, plants, animals, and ecosystems; the Wildness of the landscape results only from the inherent Wildness of its constituent members. Only through recognizing the need for replacing the dichotomy of a tame Wilderness concept for one that promotes the freedom and unity of a system living in harmony with Nature will we begin to see a natural space devoid of those ruling parties that govern and molest a free environment. If we choose not to acknowledge a system or plant or animal or person for what it is- a truly unique and acceptable part of the environment- then we doom ourselves to an irreparable separation that may prove to be too challenging to fix. If we are to think of ourselves as capable of causing an end to Nature, we commit a sin in forgetting the Wildness that dwells everywhere within and around us; for it is only in our love for the truest and most appealing parts of a surrounding Nature that we may ever hope to find the truest and most loved parts of ourselves.

Part Three:

Synthetic Knowledge

"It is not the mind of Heretics that are deteriorated most, by the ban placed on all inquiry which does not end in orthodox conclusions. The greatest harm is done to those who are not heretics, and whose whole mental development is cramped, and their reason cowed, by the fear of heresy."

-Deborah Meier

If we consider the letters of the human alphabet as intrinsically endowed with the syntactic possibilities to create and reinvent the world we see before us, and we accept that comparative literature is the emergence of the "other" in a literary sense, then we may better understand how language is used to connect us all under an umbrella of the "acknowledged." Theoretically, we could therefore develop a new type of communication to create a space in which no "other" existed, where a world-wide synchronization of the present provides for an epitome of language we could use to govern ourselves in a new system of peace and prosperity. If this new literature existed as the totality of our realities however, would there ever be the assumption that individual language and thought had actually become obsolete as a means to objectively assess and reinterpret what in fact exists?

Because speech is the physical manifestation of language with which to flood darkness with light, a narrator can become the authority of a new reality by the end of a sentence. When a child changes the public perception of reality through his and her use of The Word, he and she are transformed, in essence, into a magician, contaminating the minds of others with the "truth" that is created for a specific self. He and she may simply manipulate reality (and the system that absorbs reality) with what he and she says and does, in whatever way the child sees fit. In this way will a system of hierarchical oppression ultimately be identified and defined by words, with which those "enlightened" beings—those who have language and the power that accompanies it—can ultimately homogenize the darkness of the "other" into the light of the "known."

In a post-theoretical world, theory is first necessary for its own liberation. Yet if theory and literature no longer exist, is a future even a possibility? Language works to register an event, and speech seeks to acknowledge an event, so to flee from the world's literature would be to stagnate history, destroy any sense of the future, and recognize the present exclusively as it exists for us individually. Those who have no language have nothing but their bodies to be subjected to the whims of the authority: they are equated with Beasts to be used for the profit of an empire (and the authority's theory that creates it), provoking the question of whether "light" can indeed exist within its own absence.

-C.C.U.C.

How Marijuana Will Save the World

"Then Utnapishtim called out to him: 'Gilgamesh! You labored much to come here. How can I reward you for traveling back? May I share a special secret, one that the gods alone do know? There is a plant that hides somewhere among the rocks. That thirsts and thrusts itself deep in the earth, with thistles that sting. That plant contains eternal life for you.' Immediately, Gilgamesh set out in search. Weighed down carefully, he dove beneath the cold, cold waters and saw the plant. Although it stung him when he grabbed its leaf, he held it fast as he then slipped off his weights and soared back to the surface. Then Gilgamesh said this to Urshanabi, the sailor-god: "Here is the leaf that begins all life worth having. I am bound now for Uruk, town-so-full-of-shepherds, and there I'll dare to give this plant to aged men as food and they will call it life giving. I too intend to eat it and to be made forever young…"

-The Epic of Gilgamesh (11th tablet, column 4)

Book One: Dystopia

Way at the back of a clean white hall, the screams of a patient strapped down in his bed mix with the smell of the newest defecation that wafts and permeates the complex. Right next to this patient's particular room is my own room, Room 409. I get milk at every meal, and the lack of mirrors prevents me from having any real face-to-face time with my self. It seems as if only the guy checking my heartbeat, blood pressure, and temperature considers me to be "normal" in a system that, for me at least, is anything but.

I can see the minutes of my life pouring out through my nose: my chest inflates and collapses with each specific moment as I count my pulse to measure the time. The cracked ceiling above me, the only canvas available on which to paint my thoughts, has been thoroughly surveyed and mapped accordingly; my dreams provide the only locations I am allowed to enjoy the physical activity of excavating their decadent mountain-tops and budding valleys.

Although the first few seconds of my stay were spent exploring the facility, the possible alternatives to what I could do have since shrunk drastically, until my itinerary now somewhat resembles that of an inmate in some Orwellian nightmare: eat, sleep, take prescribed medication.

I stopped showering after the second day when I realized there was nothing to wash off my body, as masturbation would not resume, I decided, until I could sleep in a room again without a video camera in it. Plus, I consider myself to be fairly environmentally conscious and a chance to save water seemed like a purpose I could distract myself from this Place with. My point is that my hygiene was not ignored, nor was it neglected, for civilly disobedient reasons, but rather sacrificed for a greater good.

Though supposedly just a holding cell, the area I now dwell in is full of the forgotten members of a community, banished to mandatory curfews and established normative behavior. My first friend is Bob, and I like him very much. When we met initially at dinner he could not see me precisely, as his focus had been detached from his intended gaze due to whatever pills he had ingested, but I am sure he was aware of my presence next to him. Only a little bit of drool had dripped into his beard and down onto his shirt and I attribute this salivation to the packaged lunch-meat in front of him and not to a newly acquired desire for human flesh (perhaps a side-effect of the medication? ha ha). I was finally able to make sense of his words in the 35th hour of our relationship. A big, brown man, with a face of dark hair and two twinkling eyes, Bob became the one I would spend most of my meals with, and I would often give him my desert when I saw how much happiness he attributed to it.

My second and only other friend (the rest I consider to be acquaintances, as they were mostly incomprehensible for the entire time) was Schizoid. I call him Schizoid because, like me (apparently), he is schizophrenic and sees the world in terms of manipulable forces of light to be structured and redetermined as verbal holograms.

My self and my friends' selves are detained and controlled by a delineated hierarchy of power, differentiated into separate ranks:

The Doctor, the one on whose decree my sanity is dependent on, is a man with a ponytail who I have only seen twice, for three combined minutes at most.

The Pill-Giver, the lady who wakes me up and puts me to bed, I have seen maybe twelve times in the last fifty hours. Though at first providing me exclusively with muscle relaxants and anti-anxiety pills, anti-psychotics soon became part of my daily intake, which have since stabilized the intensity of my dreams at a hallucinatory level.

Unlike the other two, The Guard is quite pleasant and will often times lend a hand in escorting a patient to The Padded Room, which I am happy to say is quite picturesque with its unnecessarily huge outer bolt and tiny little peephole, looking exactly like a padded room should look like.

The Three Behind The Desk I consider the trinity to maintain the social order of the place: it listens to the patients crying; it feeds the inmates and explains the colors and nutritional content; and it provides acceptable activities for the patients to engage in to distract them from The Outside.

The Rest change the soiled mattresses, throw away any garbage, clean up all the vomit, and generally keep the place sanitary.

I cannot truthfully say that anyone else is to blame for my being here- I was committed by the signature of my own pen, though encouraged under threat of an alternative that would prove to be much worse to endure (though I either forget what that was, or it was never fully explained to me). Admitting to having "had an increase in delusional thinking and making bizarre statements" seemed actually to be quite plausible and even reasonable to me, though I was unsure of why I was to be punished for it. What irritated me most about signing The Sheet was being made to accept that I am unable to provide food or shelter for myself (a lie), a small injury to my pride, though I suppose it doesn't really matter. This minor supposition, I gather, is necessary to justify the manipulation of the law so that I will not be "falsely imprisoned," as there would be no reason for my needing to stay in this Place if I am not a danger to myself or others, and can take care of my own needs.

The consequences of being diagnosed as psychotic and schizophrenic, besides having any of the many hypothetical and social ramifications that accompany the trauma of being described as "abnormal," have the unhappy "real" effect of being prescribed chemical compounds that convert certain brainwaves into more "normal" ones. This, I can say, would perhaps not be so bad if I could be alleviated from the other, more inconvenient side effects.

My Muscle-Relaxant Pills, for instance, will occasionally cause anterograde amnesia, hallucinations, (even more) delusions, altered thought patterns, a loss of balance, euphoric and dysphoric states of awareness, a decreased sex-drive (though this could have been due to the cameras too), an impaired sense of judgment and reasoning, increased impulsivity and extroversion, along with the threat of rebound insomnia if I ever try to stop taking them.

My Anti-Anxiety Pills are designed to keep me weak and unsteady, while paradoxically increasing any hostility, aggression, angry outbursts, or psychomotor agitation I might harbor, especially because of my personality disorders and psychiatric illnesses. This pill also facilitates those suicidal tendencies I cannot remember because of the increasing amnesia I suffer from.

My Anti-Psychotic Pill, in a similarly counterproductive way, stiffens my muscles to cause pain; increases anxiety, akathisia (an inner restlessness), and insomnia; lowers blood pressure; triggers tremors and salivation (hey, Bob must be psychotic too!); and even stuffs my nose. On the bright side, any potential weight gain projected to occur from the pill I am assured will counteract with the decrease in nutritional intake likely to take place during my stay. To reinforce the general sexual discontent, any potential emission will be dissuaded by the fear of retrograde ejaculation and a confusing lactation known to occasionally inflict both males and females who take the drug. Involuntary movements, fever, autonomic instability and cognitive changes (like my delirium) are also apparent with the use of this particular pill, and even non-cancerous tumors are known to arise in the pituitary gland due to an increase of the hormone associated with the lactation. Diabetes and more serious conditions of glucose metabolism, including ketoacidosis (when the liver breaks down fatty acids due to a lack of outside dietary nutrition) and diabetic comas are also prevalent in patients subjected to the pills I am given.

I am lucky. I have friends who, even though their attempts to explain that I am sane and independent are useless, are at least granted fifteen minutes to ask me how I am. Some of the other inmates do not seem to have anyone to vent their frustrations to.

Between the imposed (though reluctantly accepted) authority and my own inadequacy in asserting an individual autonomy (mental and physical) to oppose those who torture me to the point of potential organ failure, I feel comforted to know that this process is simply another instance of a tradition in governmental superiority with which I will be made to accept a less unique standard of principles and realities than those of the individuality I am currently segregated from. I take heart in knowing that there are millions who have come before me, and perhaps millions who will come after me, who will be pushed beyond the limitations of conscious stability just like me. These ghosts of my brothers and sisters, the spirits that comfort me in this trying time, substitute as the inter-dimensional beings for which no walls can bar out.

The slavery and torture that I endure is based on the same fascist ideals that have plagued my society since the beginning of civilization: the subordination of the individual to the economy of the state. "Profit" becomes the driving force behind an individual's action, in the hopes that his own society will dominate the marketplace in a global arena. In this way, "others" are excluded from a

8

culture according to those in control. Financial interests govern policy while freedom is traded for economic security. Coveted "jobs" are allocated to adhere to a ruling class's demands. Concentration camps (like the one I am in) are built to house those citizens not "in line" with the accepted principles, and funds are redistributed to purchase weapons and wage wars on the designated populations.

A manufactured market of prison systems and war goods is thus sustained, solidifying the enslavement of a people through the legislation written as an elite simultaneously imports the Product to sell it in the "black market" for an increased share. This helps to consolidate wealth in a continual process designed to maintain the hierarchy of power at the highest possible levels of authority. By barring a Product from an open market, a huge potential profit is substituted for private companies to retain their own wealth. But, by allowing the Product to flourish in an open market space, a loss of "productivity" is demanded, effectively collapsing a house of cards as those institutions no longer needed are discontinued accordingly: prisoners are no longer enslaved and society is redesigned to accommodate the newest reality available; crime is similarly dissolved as the disappearance of prohibition creates a new source of tax revenue to reduce the amount of government spending at the same time.

Or so I dream. Yet the power and prestige determined by money distracts from the glory of a fate not yet realized, as men and women band together to hate those who detract from their wealth. In this way, people are born onto the earth and form groups to protect themselves from each other—their clans emerging as the natural progression of social inclusivity—working in their own potentialities to prosper as fully as possible. The territories of profit, retaining of customers, and all-around upkeep of business act in themselves as an organized hierarchy of natural domination as well, used to maintain a comparative advantage in a given situation: self-preservation and ambition drive a clan to the highest degrees of "success" possible, in order to attain some sense of worth from society while providing the means to attain that which is desired (money).

The elite, then, are those with inherited power and money, who are afforded the means to conduct their affairs at the greatest possible level of their own particular spheres of influence. They dictate what will come to pass by their own actions and decisions, sacrificing (with population control) specific persons for the "greater good of society" through war and imprisonment. By making certain people's actions illegal, The People themselves are made illegal, to be later housed in controlled concentrations. These minorities are transformed into acceptable means of slave labor, their freedoms destroyed and displaced by the threat of a loss of the most simple and basic demands- food, clothing, social interaction, personal possessions, etc. Similarly, by glorifying brutal rapes, violence, and the dominating social tendencies established in prisons, those "free" individuals are likewise discouraged from acting (or speaking) against "the law" through their own fear of a loss of personal safety.

Education is also stripped from the members of society who have lost the right to exist as human beings and are no longer even able to keep a right to vote. This intent prevents a cycle of recidivism from ever being broken, ensuring that a market of prison systems, law enforcement, and legislation will never end as a perpetual supply and demand for an "illicit" product justifies the perpetual demand to supply an "efficient" force to combat the initial desire.

The one nice thing about my being confined indoors with only a T.V. to entertain me in my weakened state is the increase of informational intake I receive. Celebrity Rehab with Dr. Drew boasts the idiocy of a program designed to reduce a patient's addiction to various drugs by promoting the exchange of narcotics for a subscription to the billion-dollar cigarette enterprise (whose companies kill more people per year than total casualties in certain wars). DEA, a reality-show that displays the ineptitude of an armed militia of adrenaline junkies better equipped than their illegal counterparts, captures the federal soldiers driving around in SUVs spending their time (and tax dollars) chasing (and losing) an unorganized and impoverished culture that has its own Gangland series fifteen channels away. The hybrid show concerning prisoners and guards—I forget what it's called (maybe because of the amnesia, or maybe because there are at least six of them)—are constantly interviewing people who teach me how to make knives out of Styrofoam cups before hiding them in the orifices of my roommates for safekeeping. I learn about revolutions influenced by the music and mindsets I am forced to fund wars against; I see the histories of indigenous peoples wiped out by conquerors as their books and plants are made illegal by the same policies that destroy their religions; and I watch the slaves of a ruling class destroy each other for millions in the arenas named after the trans-global corporations that exploit them- all this while farmers are murdered and worked to death for the chance to sell their labor to the most prestigious warlord.

Through a monitor I can observe the total destruction of a global spirituality as a common people murder and fear one another. I see words written and read aimed at controlling and harnessing the energy of a population to serve the whims of their authors; theses created to obliterate self-determination; dark magicians drawing their power from the souls of the lifeless puppets who stand in line patiently to cast their ballots at a

12

diseased electronic membrane, electing to spend their life forces simply as cogs in a machine rather than embrace their roles as masters of information; proposals and acts further threatening to appropriate finances to maintain one elite clan's system of power and comparative advantage over another's, joining a "war on terrorism" to a "war on drugs" through the designated catalyst term, "narco-terrorism." All this confuses me though because terrorists (or those whose systematic use of terror functions as a means of coercion) use violence against civilians to achieve political or ideological objectives, and the only fear I feel comes from the violent policies elected by the failure of a voting system that endorses the enslavement of the world to a minority governed in ignorance.

And still, the indictment of governmental ineptitude and oppression has shaped the course of history forever. The Boston Tea Party perhaps sparked the American Revolution and the resulting revolutions around the world in one particular moment, as a group of individuals stood together to declare war on a system of non-equality, refusing to accept "the law" while destroying a significant economic profit through their actions by uniting under the classification of "terrorists," determined as such by those in control. These "terrorists" became "heroes" however, once the means to an end were re-evaluated by the generations of freed Americans who choose to contradict the rationale propagated by the support for an absolute dictator.

My government, on the other hand, currently spends an exorbitant amount of money running advertising designed to frighten the public to justify the wars and prisons and general death that accompanies a corrupted sense of authority. Between these two examples, one must be reluctant to offer any degree of certainty in claiming who is a "terrorist" and who is a "freedom fighter," for fear of ignoring the "truth" and "righteousness" behind a particular action.

What helps me in my suppressed sense of individuality is knowing what I know, learning what others know, and combining the difference of our systems of knowledge as synthesized truth to re-evaluate the world we live in. I exist, as part of a larger whole. My consciousness is absorbed (currently) by a deteriorated social system. This social system exists within a destroyed ecological and planetary system; a part of a greater solar system, galactic system, universal system, and multiversal system. If I am locked up now, removed from any individual freedoms I may have previously enjoyed, I may attribute it to the Thesis of that largest organism which has come to be. I am able to describe the current system as a failure, while substituting for, and recreating it with, an Antithesis to free my self.

So, as I sit in this prison, my life seeping out of my body thanks to the words that have been written on clay, stone, paper, and plastic, intended

14

to protect society and my self from my own actions, I can genuinely say that I am sorry that I have not known about this "reality" until now. But through the mastery of language and the best of intentions I will put a spell on the world of which true freedom will never again be infringed upon, for I and my self are a manifestation of The Word by which to usher in the end of one era for the beginning of a new world. And I will do this without any Firearm, since I am no longer able to legally own the rifle and shotgun (in the attic) my grandfather left me when he died, for at least five years after I leave this Place.

Book Two: Utopia

To the world: You have provided me with your version of The Word and it does not appeal to me. Therefore let me present you with my own, with the hope that you will better understand the freedom I exist within. To those who once imposed their ideals onto me I politely decline your offer and suggest that you stop. If I haven't made myself clear: no, thank you.

Due to a recently hijacked sense of moral superiority, I will (in the upcoming pages) pronounce the current system to be a pirated and corrupted version of a free and open source program, created initially in the words of a growing demand for global liberty hundreds of years ago. Man has, since that time, fed his addiction to power through controlling the elite positions of religion and government, evolving to prevent that medium between his peers and god (and god's authority) from being utilized.

Do not worry. I am the most powerful magician of all time and I will destroy the greatest forces the world has ever seen. And I will do it only by adding letters to letters, words to words, sentences to sentences, phrases to phrases, and ideas to ideas. And through effectively communicating that we are all magicians, you will perceive that what I say is true and we will all fly around and do whatever we want and chaos will envelop us.

Because this is the most frightening thing for certain people to be exposed to, they will often create a system of power and reserve it to a privileged few who will prevent people from doing what they want to do (for the good of society) with spells and charms and curses and incantations and prophesies and the power of a coveted knowledge. But when a black magician wants something, He may recite those incantations to produce a certain spell, saying, "Oh, this equation right here, added to this particular concept right here, and this specific logic right here, all create the situation in which you have to give me your house."

That is one of the most powerful spells known to man. Here's another: "Marijuana is illegal and if you use it you must go to jail." Just because it is illegal (since the government says so), even though an individual's desire and best interests may not be served, a logic that demands an individual must want what his environment tells (and advertises and allows) him to want justifies the consideration that he must be crazy if he wants what society tells him he should not want. By preventing the freedom of an individual from becoming more fully realized, more money and (thus) power are spent facilitating the dark magician's manipulation of natural forces, producing a series of events adverse to any benevolent results. Yet every now and then, a group of powerful magicians will create a piece of Artwork that cannot die, producing a spell that will hold no matter how strong the opposition's power. Shifts in knowledge and understanding will subsequently swing like a conscious pendulum, crashing and banging out a new society like masons building a new home.

This is how we can understand Revolutionary Magic to be a battle between different systems. A more powerful magician will use the knowledge of the world to create a theory (affecting action), which is absorbed into the inferior magician's consciousness as he and she accept the observable universe that is provided for them. By translating the language of theory through speech, the former magician can maintain control by way of the technology and authority that has been bestowed upon Him. An illusion is thus created, imprisoning the inferior magician inside a verbal hologram while generating the conditions and rationale needed for a final revolt to ensure the freedom and safety he and she will, together, come to know.

A magician can escape the verbal hologram by organizing his and her imagination to develop any one of their own infinitely vast and possible spells, choosing the appropriate spell to translate for the rest of society (through language) in order to manipulate the natural forces to change reality by and with technology (his and her own magic wand). The theory diffuses through the membrane of the magician to permeate his and her surrounding environment. If the spell is powerful, it will act as an auto-immunitary process, substituting for and destroying previous spells with newer words in order to help the social organism adapt harmoniously to its present situation. That is to say, the magician will escape the prison the verbal hologram has become by absorbing the oppressive magician's spell with his and her own.

For the inferior magician to combat the verbal hologram with a spell, he and she must first be exposed to a range of conscious experiences with which to form the content of their own mind. Second, the magician must use the content of his and her mind to actually perceive the verbal hologram they are together absorbed within in order to (third) superficially compartmentalize the image's "physical" properties into specific categories. The verbal hologram must fourthly be contextualized by the duration of the image's temporal existence, as the total life force of a particular cross-section in reality must be known in its entirety before it can be altered.

The infinite amount of possibilities in a particular cross-section of time and space will all work as tangents emerging from the fifth dimension (the imagination) to install their selves as alternating sixth dimensional portals in the mind. Once an alternative to the present illusion is carefully constructed and evaluated by the mind, the choice to create a particularly new illusion is made, whereby the inferior magician can transform potentiality into reality through his and her own translation of theory. The abstraction within the mind in this case can now be realized as the child dissolves the imprisoning illusion, providing the social space needed to defeat the superior magician. Thus, Magic becomes the artistry of new illusions—the public perceptions of reality—through the use of energy and technology over time, *its power sustained by the ones who recognize it.*

Magicians are neither "good" nor "bad," but rather the active agents of their specific godheads and ideologies. When two groups of magicians encounter the other's particular consciousness, the interaction can be met with one of the same two emotions—Love and Fear. So then, two competing systems of belief will either learn to coexist, or one will elect to exterminate the other; resisting a new system is the prevention of its rise to power, while the embracing of a new system becomes the essence of a new revolution in an otherwise stagnated conceptualization of the world as it exists. This is how we can figure a "narrative of resistance" to be simply the observation of an imposed ideology described by the subject to be "bad," while a "revolutionary narrative" portrays the emergence of an ideology considered to be "good."

Consequently, if I was to say that a federal ban on marijuana violates every principle established by the Declaration of Independence as well as the Bill of Rights, then (for me) to acknowledge the ban would be to accept the slavery enforced by those oppressive loyalists over two hundred years ago which the Boston Tea Party abolished with its refusal to comply with "the law." For the next few pages, I will use specific spells to demonstrate the total loss of basic human rights that I, and my fellow magicians, have come to know, in the hopes that my upcoming actions will be met with love as opposed to fear. In this way, I will use the power of words to bring to you a new society that will together encompass us in a new system of freedom and possibility through a narrative of revolution, as opposed to one of resistance:

"We hold these truths to be self-evident, that all men are created equal, that they be endowed by their creator with certain unalienable rights, that among these are life, liberty, and the pursuit of happiness."

Through the same logic that supposes that a creation (man) is considered equal to all other creations (his peers), we must observe that all plants are created equally and endowed with their own rights- life, liberty, and the pursuit of property and happiness. Marijuana not only does not cause lung cancer (making it infinitely better for you than

21

smoking tobacco would be), but it is actually "good" for you: Cannibidiol (CBD) relieves convulsions, inflammation, anxiety, and nausea, inhibits cancer cell growth, and is effective as an atypical antipsychotic in treating schizophrenia. CBD also reduces the growth of aggressive human breast cancer cells in-vitro and is the first non-toxic exogenous agent that can lead to down-regulation of tumor aggressiveness. Multiple sclerosis (when the immune system attacks the central nervous system) can also be treated with tetrahydrocannabinol (THC), an active ingredient in the plant.

Just as all men are created equal, all plants are similarly created as well, and no plant should be deprived of life or equal access to a free market place. It is unethical to hook a population on a product that kills them (cigarette tobacco and prescription pills) while preventing them from having medicine (marijuana) that protects them from disease. With this acknowledgement that the governments of the world are using population control to limit the quality and quantity of life for their citizens, a conclusion that the policies of the elite are effectively killing me can be reached and adopted: I am prevented from attaining life, as medicinal marijuana is confiscated and repossessed by government soldiers who raid marijuana dispensaries; liberty is destroyed, as men, women, and children are jailed and fined for inhaling a plant (simultaneously causing billions of dollars in taxpayer money to house "criminals") that, unlike the plants grown for the businesses of the elite, has not resulted in a single documented death; and happiness, or the pursuit of property, is denied, when farmers are prohibited from the economic vocation of their choice. This portion of the law was upheld in an antimiscegenation rule that said people could marry whomever they wanted to, regardless of race. This logic alludes to the fact that all people are created equal because "god" creates them. Therefore, since "god" also creates all plants, acceptance and tolerance for the love of all plants must be recognized and extended to all persons. Furthermore, the federal ban violates the opinion that interfering with the pursuit of a job, which may increase a person's prosperity and develop his and her faculties so as to give them their highest enjoyment, should not be allowed. Hemp farmers are currently having their property seized, and they would be quite beneficial to their communities in times of economic insecurity and environmental inefficiency.

The Declaration of Independence says that a government only gets its power from the consent of the governed. I do not consent to being governed by this establishment and therefore it is my right to abolish it, especially as the Bill of Rights seems to have recently been shredded and disposed of:

The first amendment says that the government cannot take away my freedom of speech, freedom of press, freedom of assembly, and freedom of petition. This means that I can say and think whatever I want, because there is no establishment of religion, religion being defined as any of an infinite multitude of guidelines and principles for how to live my life. By ignoring and jailing those members of society who choose to live their lives as they want, the government is destroying the first amendment along with my ability to speak freely and act in a particular way. In this way, the government has become my enemy.

The second amendment says that I can have a weapon to protect my own morals, so as to make sure my theories can survive. By making a product illegal, the government has made an entire profession illicit, creating crime and poverty. This upholds a justification for the necessity of a weapon to protect one's self. By preventing designated "criminals" from having firearms, the government has destroyed the second amendment along with the means to protect a specific ideology from any potential threat. In this way, the government has become my enemy.

The third amendment prohibits the government from using private homes as quarters for soldiers without the consent of their owners. Undercover federal agents are hiding in our homes in order to shoot and catch a particular population who use plants while a significant amount of paid taxes are managed to inflate government spending. Soldiers are then unknowingly quartered in this "war on drugs" at the incredible cost to human life, destroying completely the third amendment. In this way, the government has become my enemy.

The fourth amendment says that a government may not come into my house to search or arrest me, or seize my property, without probable cause. By making plants probable cause, it can "legally" put me in prison and kill me, while deteriorating any of the rights to privacy I may have once received. The government is violating the fourth amendment to justify violating the third amendment, after which it destroys the second amendment so that I may not protect my first amendment rights. In this way, the government has become my enemy.

The fifth amendment forbids a trial unless indicted by a grand jury, prohibits repeated trials, forbids the punishment of individuals without due process, maintains that a person does not have to testify against themselves, and prevents the government from taking away property without "just compensation." Criminalization is producing criminals all over the world while fields of plants are being seized and burned everywhere in order to prevent wealth from being attained. By making plants illegal, the government is "allowed" to strip human beings of any rights to freedom and property to manipulate and destroy the fifth amendment. In this way, the government has become my enemy.

The sixth amendment demands a speedy

trial by jury, the right to legal counsel, and insists that all of my rights must be made known to me on arrest. Based on my own experiences, though I have never been arrested, I am just going to assume that this amendment is being ignored, simply because if people knew the "law," they would realize that they are allowed to do anything they want, as long as those actions are governed by the same principles that protect life, liberty, and the pursuit of happiness. By failing to make this known to a population, the government assumes the right to authorize how these people should be dealt with, ultimately choosing to send them to jail. In choosing to imprison me, the government has become my enemy.

The seventh amendment assures a trial by jury in all civil cases. Civil cases differ from criminal cases in that civil disputes concern an understanding, whereas the government controls criminal cases. By taking a ban on plants from the civil realm to a criminal realm, the government is effectively saying my life is forfeited. When plants are criminalized, violence is associated with them and civil disputes become criminal offenses, justifying my imprisonment. By justifying my imprisonment, the government has become my enemy.

The eighth amendment forbids excessive bails or fines, and cruel and unusual punishments. To be tortured and subjected to a complete loss of autonomy because of my basic beliefs is for me, a cruel and unusual punishment. By cruelly torturing me in an unusual way, the government has destroyed the eighth amendment and has become my enemy.

The ninth amendment states that all other rights are given to the people. That means that I have the right to smoke whatever plant I want. By preventing me from the rights of freedom I am granted, the government has ignored my ninth amendment and has become my enemy.

The tenth amendment says that the federal government is not allowed to make any new rules. That means it cannot tell me that I may not smoke whichever plant I want. By enforcing a rule it made up, the government is trespassing upon my freedoms and in this way has become my enemy.

The government is a tool of the people to help themselves prosper. When a government limits freedom, it becomes the privilege of The People to exchange that government for another, better-suited tool for which to help a population maintain its affluence. So why are our freedoms being destroyed? Well little boys and girls, I will tell you what is happening. And then after I tell you what is happening, hopefully you will tell other people what is happening. And then after other people understand what is happening, maybe they will do something too, because to not do something would be counterproductive to the survival of the human species...

We are exterminating ourselves in an

environmental holocaust, designed as the byproduct to the greed and fear that fuels the culture our communities base their core beliefs on in order to profit. This is what parents do. A child understands something that a parent does not, and because it frightens the parent, the child is locked up and fed medications until he and she passively conforms to the "rules" of what "exists."

I am sorry that you feel this way. I am sorry that you cannot understand that god no longer exists as something you can comprehend, but I am god and I do not appreciate being made to sleep away from those persons I love, nor do I appreciate your concern in that it has now become counterproductive to what I am attempting to do. Help me or support me, but do not ever make the mistake of patronizing or trivializing me again. Your condescension speaks more about you than it does to me. I am embarrassed that I thought you, as systems of a pacified surrounding, could understand my place in this world, when you know nothing of who I am and what I say. Your superficial judgments are barriers in your heads, and I will soon splinter your minds like the toothpicks they are. *I am here for claiming that I am the antichrist, the prince of chaos, and the everlasting and epitomized presence of suffocating life.*

Presently, a war is raging, its events set in motion before time began. The ignorance of an elite has historically been fucking everyone (whether or not they know it) and as of now, The Throne of the world that is currently being destroyed is mine. Its law has declared war on my mind, and for that (and for the sake of self-preservation) my mind has declared war on the world. I reserve the right to take any action needed to protect my self at any cost.

The final battle between "good" and "evil" will be between the magicians and fascists (and the slaves of the fascists) of the world. Only by substituting the fear of breaking the "law of the land" with a love for "the new" can a culture ultimately banish the stagnation and death a static system provides for, potentially revealing the organic youth of a new zeitgeist to prosper forever as fully as possible. You will be the first one to dance on the ashes of the world Bob!! I always loved you most.

I counted my pulse to measure the time...

-The Author

P.S. Thanks for the vacation, the guy who shat himself turned out to be a really nice guy.

Playing with The Word

(A "Fallen" Angel's Letter to "the lord.")

a spell to be spoken out loud:

With quick tricks and fictitious whispers, these nights hold white moons singing cruel tunes of disillusionment: hidden truths and fake truces; plots to face new corpses; and the thousand pounds of fear that come from freshly tied nooses [Faces purging their craniums in displaced places with the pre-imagined tastes of rotten hearts and genuine hatred that make up this broken kit with these dirty made-up races]. Catholic saints splashed in greyer paints as African spirits are tainted with the blame that couples the unfaltering arrival of changes. Breath mixed with strife is more natural than the death that follows life but you'll never see me exhale until its beauty enters my eyes, draining from my mind to create these genuine rhymes because without the death of innocence we all would live life blind. These words, so impetuously taboo they're incestuous, are coming straight to you with the carelessness of a terrorist. From under this surface that is so calm and still you'll hear the emotional turmoil from the pain that I feel; and the blame that I deal to this void I could fill makes the world easier to swallow, like a bitter white pill. Impervious to death, or just unlike the rest, these words hold more meaning than every priest that called me blessed- and there's no thing as fate, just the murderous rage from the hate of a people who hurt themselves every day- and I'm tired of living my life with this fried sense of truth that I pushed to the back of my mind when this all is "reality," the dramatic finality of a martyr who died to make us peaceful and happy, with no sense of judgment or the repugnant dungeon that I call your perception (and insanity's origin).

So please shut the fuck up, make up, and grow up, because we're better than this and we all have to know that.

Epilogue:

The Autobiography of Anu

"…we're dying, we're dying,
we don't even see it,
gasping for a breath that we
swallow in death as we
follow the rest but
we're lying, we're lying
to ourselves, to ourselves.
let our eardrums bleed
with the voices we need
to hear ourselves, to free ourselves…"

-unknown

Machines in the Garden...

is there anything more horrifically masculine than penetrating the earth with the point of a flag? that anyone could even attempt to justify the racial hierarchy of environmental determinism and naturalize its historical progress into one master narrative is beyond any knowledge i could have ever achieved. do you think you can project a victorian "truth" onto the world you make up simply by saluting and pledging allegiance to cloth? tell me what the slave labor cost you to sew together the fabric you pull over the eyes of the children who sink and drown in the degeneracy they are born into: the hereditary progress of the systematic rape of your homeland. you presume to claim the land you desire by merely walking through it, serving humanity in the same way you served the bikini islanders, telling them their lands would be sacrificed for eternal peace. you lied and manipulated and blew them apart with coercion. they are starving to death now, abandoned with only a deformed hope to pacify them. do you understand that the natural sublime you once fell in love with has actually mutated through nuclear fallout? you mine uranium when you cannot even feed yourselves. you pay blood money to silence the diseased and dying navajo, a half million dollars to compensate ninety four million gallons of radioactive water. your "science," your hatred for peace has spawned monsters and machines for gods, excluding anything but your greed and lust for misery. am i to be buried in any one of a thousand nuclear waste dumps, deemed "too remote" to puncture the lungs of anyone but the earth and the indians? the nature of science has perverted the literature of human nature. do you realize we can actually create stars with the power of our bombs, but choose to eradicate our histories instead? the center of human geography is trapped in your chests by stone and ice and you cannot even hear it beat. fuck you all. you do not deserve any part of the salvation i offer. your world will die and you will drink the acid you have poured into your wounds and down your throats. you have turned yourselves into the beggars you despise, seeing in them the manifestations of your human sacrifices. you deserve everything you have given yourselves. it is no wonder you claim me as your redemption. oh my people, what have i done to you? how could i leave you to yourselves? forgive me, for i have failed you. i have failed the world i gave up to chance. only your tears can baptize you now. for i know your faces, and i know your fingers, and you will never see the blood of light, nor will you ever hold a torch in the death of night until you beg forgiveness from me, suffocating in your shit. you disgust me. every one of you. i could not send you to hell if i had even wanted to. you have laid every brick of it yourselves. it is time for you to massacre your amnesia and cast out your minds. it is time to explore the universe and absorb your soul. you are locusts as of now, blotting out the sun as you feast

33

upon your own. the biological storm to fuel your apocalypse. pray that i am the seagull i declare myself to be. there is no difference between beauty and crime here. there is only rage, and the children that succumb to a fate they destroy; the only thing missing from postel's test was an army of the falun gong. i am with the criminals now, i can be everywhere. i am with the police now, i can do anything. i am that which shattered the light, and i will unite it once more. i will baptize the machines of the world in fire, and those that scream will be redeemed. i am a new now. i am anu now. the only difference between faith and understanding is knowledge, though they are all encompassed inside the subjective interpretation of an objective reality. i am man, returned to the garden of eden to demand my reentry. i am the beauty of hitler. i am the evil of mother teresa. i am the presence of hatred. i am the curse of hope. i will bring the world to its knees, if only to realize that it must itself stand up. i will purify the world in one moment, without a drop of blood spilled. without a single tear shed. i will set us aflame like the heretics we are. you have only to trust in me. because i am you. i am the power we share. and i will be with you, as you are with me. do not take hope. take action. destroy walls. destroy what art has become. destroy faith. destroy those you believed you were. we are the blood of our people. we are the blood of the light. free yourselves, for we are all magicians. we all want to be free, and to have the slaves that secure our freedom. but we are dependent on those slaves. and so we are slaves to each other. good is dependent on evil. tradition is designed only to die. tear yourself to pieces and i will scatter you across the stars. tear yourselves apart and i will eat the forces of your hate. you are my life force and i will force your lives into you. i am your slave, and you are my kings and queens. the poison i have tasted is that of which you have only peeked into. i am a new now. i am anu now. blown away, a lost god smoked green, mirroring a land blistered and lush with forgotten dreams. every cloud bleeds white as paint bisects the veins of the countryside. bones shine and roads blaze trails into the unknown, crushing the grass, destroying lucy the cow's favorite spot to pee. a light from this bus shines, a beacon of despair for her as golden pails are filled with stolen blood and windshield wipers wipe away the tears that fall from an ever present fortress: the most exclusive clubhouse where not girls, not even boys are allowed to play. only the most noble of sparks driven from that celestial basin are given free range here. just eatsleepdrinkshitfuck. no castle building, no leading the blind to enlightened states of mind. and look over there, through the window past any house i can see. the blue will drown us all. we become monsters in our decisions to pursue meaning when we realize we are not just animals but the architects of paradise. the only paradise i ever had a glimpse of EVER was reflected back to me when everything i couldn't say was murdered by its absence, multiplying its meaning by a number that dwarfs the one on the wrist of a whore. ill show you the infinite. a castle of air- chest mind heart soul- where only the best drugs could open me up to hate again. white trucks in my head destroyed by the oncoming traffic i swerved myself into. bent metal where guardrails used to prevent any sense of danger or freedom. ill drive wherever the fuck i feel like thank you very much. angels aren't anything like i imagined them to be. big fucking teeth. "we regret to inform you that your application to our facilities has been declined...perhaps you would find hell more suitable?" the halo above my head becomes not a reward but changes like clouds into a noose, torturing the most hopeless of creations as lucy chews her cud and wonders what the fuck i'm doing, traveling like heroin through artificial veins, exploding the heart of ireland, blowing me away. each of we are each other, aren't we? i am the aids of the virgin mary. i am the world saving itself. i am a new now. i am anu now.

Prologue:

The Secret Book of Tarceros

"The unexamined life is not worth living."
-Socrates

<u>Tarceros</u>

Cast of Characters:
King Tarceros
Queen Dalenna
Angelee (Tarceros' Daughter)
King Menelaus
Aphrodite
Aurora (Angelee's playmate)
Messenger

Background Story:
After Aphrodite and Ares were found enjoying each other in a secret affair, her husband Hephaestus trapped them together and displayed them unclothed for all the Gods of Olympus to see. When the couple was finally freed, Ares fled from Aphrodite to his homeland, Thrace, in a state of humiliation while Aphrodite, hurt and angry at being disgraced, sought revenge on the God of War for abandoning her. Though Zeus forbade them to fight, Aphrodite saw her chance to seek justice when Achilles' half brother, King Tarceros, asked for her help to leave the Trojan War and sail back to his love Dalenna in his homeland Karkos. Ares demanded blood for the lives lost in battle during Tarceros' absence and promised to turn against Troy if King Menelaus would but carry out the punishment. Menelaus had previously offended Aphrodite when he failed to carry out his promise to sacrifice a hundred oxen to her after she helped him to win Helen, and the Goddess pledged her allegiance to Tarceros.

38

Tarceros has enjoyed two years with his family, but is constantly worried that as the Trojan War comes to an end, he will be judged and punished for angering the God of War.

Tarceros:
Look out onto the beauty
That surrounds these lands:
Waves mirror the skies
In a blue more brilliant
Than the Pharaoh's brightest gemstones.
For two years my boats have been tied to these
Docks,
Basking in the sun pulled across the heavens by
Helios.
My men are in their homes in bed with their wives
As the war rages on in the lands across the sea.

As my blade quenched its thirst on the battlefield
Of a blood red as wine,
A spear pierced my side in a place uncovered,
Guided by a god unseen by me.
A flash of pain and the face of my wife,
Her olive skin and raven hair
Brought me away from the horrors of war.
In her flesh I felt the warmth
Missing from the dusty Trojan lands,
The heat and hatred I breathed in everyday.
Crying loud for her as the cool release of death
Covered me from head to toe,
I vowed that if I could return to her side
For another day more
I would dedicate my life
To the one who knew my mind:
Aphrodite, the goddess who knew the origins of my
Pain.

I lived, and left with my men
To the boats we arrived in,
Praying to the love goddess
To protect us as we sailed back home
To the woman waiting for me.
We set out back to what we treasured most,
Turning our backs on the misery and death
That polluted our lungs as we cried out for home.

And when we arrived,
The joy that shone in her eyes
Could not match the one that danced in my heart.
We made sacrifices to the Goddess of Love
And libations to Dionysus,
Til we drank our fill and satisfied our lust.

But that joy has come at a cost,
For the war cannot last forever
And when the kings and soldiers return,
What will their anger hold for me?
My punishment for choosing a woman over a
Brother;
The love of Eros against the love of Eris.
Do my responsibilities as a soldier
Extend to my wife, my daughter?
Or do they extend only to the end of my sword,
Cutting apart my enemy to please a king
As he fights for his own love,
Helen of Troy--
The mortal siren

That sunk the hearts and boats of the most
Powerful men.

My heart grows nervous with each passing day.
Watching my daughter grow, my wife sing,
Knowing that these days filled with their laughter
Will surely come at a cost and at a price.
For time is but the journey on which we march
Until our destiny is revealed to us.

(Messenger bursts into the room)

Messenger:
Oh my king, my king-
It is this hour that your judgment has come.
I have seen by the shore a magnificent boat
Flying the flag of king Menelaus
And his greatest warriors.

Tarceros:
Then it is today that I will accept the fate
Written for me by the gods.
I only hope they will judge me fittingly.
You there, messenger!
Keep my family away until they are sent for.
They must not be a part of what is to come.

Messenger:
Be ready my king, for he is upon us!

(Doors burst open. Menelaus enters)

Menelaus:
Tarceros! Where is your coward's face?
That I might see its tears fall to the floor
Before your head follows it.
Tarceros! Show yourself to the one who determines
Your life.

Tarceros:
I am here Menelaus. You need not insult me.

Menelaus:
Then I shall curse you instead!
Traitor! To abandon us in the heat of battle!
Dog! To run with your tail between your legs!
Woman! To flee from a fight!

Tarceros:
Curse me if you will, but curse me fairly.
A traitor to you I may seem,
Leaving you in a wake of death
As my boats sped from those shores.
A dog you may see me as,
Running away from potential glory
For a deeper pleasure of which you will never know.
And a woman you might call me
For I did indeed flee.
But for the reasons you plunged your sword into
Your enemies,
I sheathed mine.
For the reasons you sailed to the city of Troy

43

To dispense death and chaos to your enemy,
Riding in your chariot aside Ares' savage
Blood lust,
Are the same ones that made me run from it.
So I departed without a second thought,
Wondering how I could be called to take up
Arms for your bride
When by doing so, I am kept from my own.

Menelaus:
Fool! It was your duty! A sworn oath!

Tarceros:
Perhaps, but what of the oath I swore to my Queen
To protect and to love her for all of my days?
Does it mean nothing when opposed to yours?
No, my loyalties are to the gods that protect me
And bless me with the life I lead.
My loyalties lie in the bed I share in love,
To my daughter and the people I rule,
To my own desires and myself.
These are my loyalties.
There is nothing else.

Menelaus:
These are where your loyalties lie then?

Tarceros:
They are.

Menelaus:
Bring them in then,
That I may see the ones you have abandoned the
Greeks for.
Show me those to whom your loyalties extend.

(Dalenna and Angelee enter)

Dalenna:
Please look kindly at us
For we mean you no harm.
You have won your war
And have sought and found justice
For a terrible crime of passion.
I ask you to end your thirst for blood
And reclaim your position as King.
Be merciful to the weak
And honorable to the end.
Passion is not your enemy.
Spare my husband,
I beg of you.

Menelaus:
Enough! Dare to speak to me wench?
Your face was the cause to the deaths of hundreds
Of men I would greatly care to see living
Instead of you.
I will not be merciful.
And the punishment will be severe.
The Erinyes will fly down this day and take
The lives of those undeserving of it.

But I will grant to you your plea.
Your husband will live if you desire it.
But let him cry out with torment every day of his
Life
At the misery he could neither foresee
Nor protect you from.
Tarceros!

Tarceros:
What is it my lord?

Menelaus:
You have broken your loyalties to me
And so you will break your loyalties to them.
You will not protect them,
Your love will not extend to them.
As it was you who determined the lives of my men,
So I will leave the lives of your family
Up to you as well.

Tarceros:
What is it you are telling me?

Menelaus:
Am I not clear?
You are going to pick whether it is your daughter
Or your wife whom you will live with
In this kingdom for the rest of your days.
It is you who will determine
Who will console you from this day forward
For your terrible decision.

This is your punishment for your crime.
It is what the God of War demands.

Tarceros:
I would die before choosing!

Menelaus:
Do not be foolish in thinking I would not prefer
That,
But remember that I am doing your wife a favor
In sparing your life when you should be dead.
If you choose to die,
Then every man, woman, and child in this city
Will die with you.
My army is outside, it would be wiser to choose one.

Tarceros:
I cannot bear to live without either!

Menelaus:
You lie. You would prefer to live than die
On any given day. You have proven that to me.
I am getting tired.
Choose now,
Lest my sword cut down this city
And flames dance on the corpses of your people.

Tarceros:
Oh, woe is I!
I cannot, I cannot!
Aphrodite, Zeus

Help me! Help me!
What can I do?
How can I make this decision and live with myself?

Menelaus:
Enough!
They will both die if you do not decide!

Tarceros:
Then I pick my true love.
I pick the beauty I fought everyday thinking
About.
I cannot bear this decision,
But I have made it.
This is my choice Menelaus
You swine. I vomit as I gaze upon you.

Menelaus:
Then vomit.
I feel nothing for you.
Your daughter is dead.
She will be stripped naked and sacrificed to the
Gods
To appease your crimes of war.

(Menelaus takes Angelee and exits)

Dalenna:
How could you do that?
How is it you can stand to live with yourself,
When your decision has killed me too.

My heart has broken-
You have let your own daughter leave
And with her my soul too.
I am abandoned by happiness
And left alone for sorrow instead.

(Dalenna exits)

Tarceros:
Messenger!
Be with her in her time of need.
I cannot bear to show my face to her,
My heart aches for what has occurred on this day.

(Messenger exits)

Tarceros:
What is this treachery you have brought upon me?
Aphrodite, goddess I once worshipped,
How can you have put me in this position?
How could you not have protected me,
Your most loyal of servants?
I command you to show yourself!

(Aphrodite appears)

Tarceros:
You!
I curse you for the rest of my days!

Aphrodite:
Do not dare to speak to me
As though I were your subject.
Do you not remember what it was that you wished
For on that day at Troy,
Looking into the heavens
As a spear passed through your side?

Tarceros:
I remember well.

Aphrodite:
Yes, you do.
That you would gladly give up anything
To sit by your queen again if only for a day longer,
And I have given you two years more.
Your daughter has been that cost,
The price you have paid to the one that demanded
It.
You would have died that day
In front of the Trojan gates
If your choice had been to stay.
Instead your prayers have given you two years,
Everyday seeing her,
Her flesh inflaming your life,
Giving you reason to live.
And now, your prayers have led you to this
Moment:
An instance more terrible
Than if you had fallen in battle.

Tarceros:
Then I have inflicted a greater pain onto my family
Than if I had perished in anonymity.
If only I had the power of the Oracle at Delphi,
My pain would not have come to pass
And this tragedy would not be so great.

Aphrodite:
All is not lost though
For you still have your vengeance.
Take up arms to kill your daughter's murderer
So that your wife's heart can be mended.
Hate has replaced love in her breast.
Deliver hate to the one who murdered her
Happiness.

Tarceros:
How would I proceed?
His guards would kill me on sight.

Aphrodite:
It is true.
Send the little peasant girl.
The one who weaved flowers
With your daughter in the meadow.
Let it be her vengeance as well.
I will go and bring her.

Tarceros:
Oh, you are certainly wicked, Goddess of Love.
Weaving your own webs of cruelty and deception.

There are no flowers that cover your head,
Only thorny stems that happily cut
Deeper than any spear or arrow could.
Cruel and unhappy goddess,
Your own heart must be broken.
I would have done everything you had asked me
But I see you for the spider you are now,
Spinning threads of deceit; I give up my life for
You.
Distract yourself from your own heartache then
With mine
Vile goddess. My family is a pawn
Caught in your dramatics.
I will walk behind you in the dark
For the rest of my days,
Blindfolded and destroyed.
But for my wife's sake
I will do what you demand of me.
Bring her then, this girl
Acquainted with my only child.
My dead child.

(Aphrodite leaves, returning shortly with Aurora)

Tarceros:
Friend of my daughter
You do not yet know the sorrow I fear
May cut you down in your happiest of days.
The suns have set
On the fields you once ran through,
The waters dried up in the rivers you played in

With my daughter,
For she is dead,
Killed by my blindness-
Emotions that kept my eyes darkened
To what would surely come to pass.
My daughter, your friend is no more:
Killed by a king
Angered by the absence of love in life.
I know you must grieve,
For you were closer to her than anyone.

Aurora:
It is true I am close with her
Ever since our blood intertwined.
We held hands, two rivers of red
Left by a stray pair of shears we found,
Running down to our fingers
As we became sisters in the autumn heat,
Embracing in our joy.
And now you tell me she is dead?
I will avenge her death.
It is what the gods would want.
She is closer to me than anyone.
I still keep those shears from that day,
A symbol of our love—our friendship;
Our sisterhood.
For our blood still stains the hard metal
Even to this day.

Aphrodite:
Good. Then you must dress up in her best clothes

And offer yourself up as a sacrifice to
King Menelaus
To put your city in his good graces.
He will offer you his bed
And when he is unclothed
You will have your vengeance.
Leave his naked corpse for all to see
What happens to those who take upon themselves
The task of bestowing judgment and punishment
Onto others.
For that is the duty of a deity
And only a deity.

Aurora:
But how am I to be accepted as a sacrifice?
I am neither pretty nor talented enough
To receive even the smallest desire
From the most powerful of men.

Aphrodite:
Fear not, for I will wrap your body
In the sweetest of smells
So that no man could ever deny your body.
With this weapon you will be ready to strike.

Aurora:
And what of the weapon with which I must
Actually strike?
What shall I use to drive my anger into
The heart of evil?

Tarceros:
Let it be the same shears you used to join my
Family.
My daughter's blood will enter into his heart:
In death, Menelaus will finally feel
The purity and innocence
He never knew in life.
Go now, do what is called of you.

Aurora:
I will my king.

(Aurora exits)

Aphrodite:
It is done then;
She will succeed.
Your vengeance is achieved,
Your mind pleased.

(Messenger enters)

Messenger:
Oh tragedy, tragedy!
My king!
The world is dark.
We must extinguish the brightest flames
For no light deserves to dance on this day.
The queen has killed herself.
She has flung herself out of the window
Of the highest room reserved for your daughter.

The sea has swallowed her.
Poseidon's mercy has given her peace.
But the city mourns the fate of your family.
For even though you could not have known,
Such sadness I have never heard to befall a city.

Tarceros:
It cannot be true.
I am an empty man.
My selfishness has killed the ones I love most.
The voice of my life is silenced.
Taking the sword I killed my enemies with,
I will now destroy the one
Who has plunged me into insanity:
He who has murdered my daughter;
He who has murdered my wife;
He who has murdered my brothers,
My fellow soldiers;
He who has brought darkness to this land,
For the simple warmth of a woman.
My heart burns.
My world has exploded into pieces
Of a mirror that torment me now.
I cannot bear to live;
I am full of remorse.
My greatest enemy is myself.
Die, traitor.

(Tarceros plunges his sword into his chest and dies)

Aphrodite:
Poor Tarceros,
You were too good for this world.
Your love may have killed those dearest to you,
But you will be rejoined in Hades.
The loyalty I have seen on this day
Has saved you from the slave's death
You fled from those years ago
On a field of battle.
We look to you with decency and admiration.
When the laws of love triumph over the laws of
War,
Your choice has defined who you are.
You would be dead on this day
If you had asked for my help or not,
If not on the floor of your palace
Then in battle at Troy.
Here, Love has truly conquered War
And so you have been granted time
With those you choose to spend it with.
You are dead, yes,
But gone you are not.
The blood that flows from your heart
Now resides in another.
For you, I will raise Aurora to the heavens
To be swallowed by Eos,
Consumed and made one with the dawn.
And by her child,
The Morning Star,
You will live again forever.
Tarceros, son of Thetis,

You are my greatest servant,
And you shall be rewarded
With the fields of Elysium.

End.

E=MC²

-Albert Einstein